A QUICK GUIDE:
Shorting

DAMIEN SOITOUT

DEDICATION

To every single one of those who are passionate enough to risk it all in order to improve their lives, raise their standards, and be the one who breaks the pattern.

CONTENT

ACKNOWLEDGEMENTS

To my daughters Dayna, Angela and Chayli, may this book be a testament to the work I never give up on doing with the sole purpose of always providing the life you deserve.

And to all these wonderful persons who believe in me; to my love, Valeriia, who inspired me to write these pages because of her legendary curiosity which never ceases to inspire me. One question from you moves forces I never suspected were hiding within me. Thank you.

INTRODUCTION

Short-selling, a strategy often regarded as the antithesis of conventional investing, involves a distinctive process that requires a keen understanding of market dynamics. Let's unravel the intricacies of how short-selling works and the strategic dance investors undertake in this financial maneuver.

At its core, short-selling begins with an investor identifying an asset, frequently stocks, that they believe is overvalued or poised for a price decline. The process kicks off with the investor borrowing the chosen asset from a broker, with the intention of returning it at a later date. This borrowed asset is then promptly sold on the open market.

The critical element of short-selling lies in the anticipation of a subsequent drop in the price of the borrowed asset. The investor, having sold the asset at its current, possibly inflated, price, now waits for the opportune moment to repurchase the same asset. The ultimate goal is to buy it back at a lower price than the one at which it was initially sold, thereby turning a profit.

PART 1

WHAT IS SHORT-SELLING?

In the dynamic world of finance, short-selling, often referred to as "shorting," is a strategy that allows investors to profit from the decline in the value of an asset. While it can be a valuable tool for portfolio management, understanding the risks associated with short-selling is crucial for any investor navigating the complex terrain of financial markets.

Short-selling, a financial strategy often shrouded in mystery, is a practice that involves a unique dance with market dynamics. At its essence, short-selling can be defined as the strategic act of selling borrowed assets with the anticipation that their market value will experience a decline. The objective is clear: to repurchase these assets later at a lower price, ultimately generating a profit for the investor.

Here's a breakdown of the key components encapsulated in the definition of short-selling:

1. Selling Borrowed Assets
Short-selling begins with the investor borrowing a specific quantity of assets

from a broker or another market participant. These assets can take various forms, but stocks are a common choice. The act of borrowing is typically facilitated through a margin account, where the investor provides collateral to secure the loan.

2. Anticipation of Value Decrease

The core belief in short-selling is the expectation that the value of the borrowed assets will decrease over a specific period. This anticipation is grounded in the investor's analysis of market conditions, company fundamentals, and other relevant factors that might influence the asset's price negatively.

3. Buy Back at a Lower Price

Having sold the borrowed assets in the open market, the short-seller patiently waits for the opportune moment. The goal is to repurchase the same quantity of assets at a later date when their market value has decreased. By buying back at a lower price than the initial selling price, the short-seller aims to capitalize on the price difference.

4. Profit Generation

The ultimate objective of short-selling is profit generation. The profit is realized when the short-seller sells the borrowed assets at a higher price than the price at which they repurchase them. This difference, accounting for transaction costs and other fees, represents the net gain for the investor.

5. Inverse Nature of Gain/Loss

Unlike traditional investing, where profits are earned by buying low and selling high, short-selling operates in an inverse manner. Profits are generated by selling high and buying low. This inversion adds a layer of complexity and requires a distinct set of analytical skills and market awareness.

6. Risk and Reward Balancing Act

Short-selling is a high-stakes endeavor, and its success hinges on the delicate balance of risk and reward. The potential for unlimited losses amplifies the risk, emphasizing the need for careful consideration, strategic timing, and ongoing monitoring of market conditions.

In summary, short-selling is a strategic financial maneuver where investors leverage borrowed assets with the expectation of a price decline. This unique approach to the markets adds dynamism to investment strategies but demands a nuanced understanding of risk factors and an astute ability to navigate the complexities of market movements. It is a practice that, when approached with diligence and a thorough understanding of market dynamics, can provide investors with a distinctive tool in their financial toolkit.

Importance of Understanding Short-Selling

In the ever-evolving landscape of financial markets, where dynamism and complexity reign, investors find themselves navigating a myriad of strategies to safeguard and enhance their portfolios. Among these strategies, the understanding of short-selling emerges as a crucial skill, providing investors with a nuanced perspective and the ability to make informed decisions. Let's explore the significance of comprehending the mechanics of short-selling in today's financial environment:

1. Diversification of Investment Strategies
Understanding short-selling adds a valuable dimension to an investor's toolkit, allowing for diversification beyond traditional long-only strategies. By incorporating short-selling techniques, investors gain the flexibility to profit not only from market upswings but also from downturns. This diversification enhances the resilience of portfolios in the face of varying market conditions.

2. Risk Mitigation and Portfolio Protection
Short-selling serves as a risk mitigation tool. In times of market uncertainty or bearish trends, the ability to profit from falling asset prices acts as a hedge, offering a counterbalance to potential losses in long positions. Investors who comprehend short-selling can strategically deploy this technique to protect their portfolios from significant downturns.

3. Enhanced Market Awareness
Grasping the mechanics of short-selling cultivates a heightened awareness of market dynamics. Investors become attuned to not only the factors

influencing asset values in an upward trajectory but also those contributing to potential declines. This comprehensive understanding empowers investors to make proactive decisions based on a holistic view of market conditions.

4. Informed Decision-Making

As financial markets continue to evolve, the ability to make informed decisions becomes paramount. Investors who understand short-selling can navigate the complexities of both bullish and bearish market scenarios. This knowledge enables them to strategically enter and exit positions, optimizing their investment decisions for maximum effectiveness.

5. Adaptability to Market Trends

Short-selling proficiency fosters adaptability to changing market trends. Investors can pivot their strategies based on evolving economic indicators, geopolitical developments, and industry-specific factors. This adaptability ensures that investors are not solely reliant on traditional investment approaches but can adjust their positions to capitalize on emerging opportunities or mitigate risks.

6. Risk and Reward Evaluation

The understanding of short-selling facilitates a nuanced evaluation of risk and reward. Investors can assess the potential risks associated with short-selling, such as unlimited losses, and weigh them against the potential rewards. This risk-conscious approach guides investors in making balanced decisions that align with their risk tolerance and overall financial goals.

7. Preventing Overvaluation and Bubbles

Short-selling plays a crucial role in preventing market overvaluation and the formation of asset bubbles. Investors proficient in short-selling can act as a check against irrational exuberance, contributing to market efficiency. This understanding promotes a healthier and more sustainable financial ecosystem.

The importance of understanding short-selling extends beyond its role as a strategy; it becomes a tool for investors to navigate the complexities of modern financial markets. As markets continue to evolve, those equipped with the knowledge of short-selling mechanics are better positioned to adapt, mitigate risks, and make informed decisions that contribute to the long-term success of their investment portfolios.

PART 2

MECHANISM OF SHORT-SELLING

Short-selling operates as a financial maneuver that involves a distinctive set of steps, creating a strategic dance with market dynamics. This mechanism offers investors the opportunity to profit from falling asset prices. Let's delve into the intricacies of how short-selling works:

How to start short-selling?

1. Identifying the Asset
The journey into short-selling commences with the investor identifying a specific asset, often stocks, that they believe is overvalued or poised for a price decline. This selection is grounded in thorough research, market analysis, and a conviction that the asset's value is likely to decrease in the near future.

2. Borrowing the Asset
Once the target asset is identified, the investor approaches a broker to borrow a predetermined quantity of the chosen asset. This borrowing process is facilitated through a margin account, where the investor provides collateral to secure the loan. The borrowed assets are then promptly transferred to the investor's account.

3. Selling in the Open Market

With the borrowed assets in hand, the investor enters the market with the intent to sell them. This selling action creates a short position, effectively placing a bet that the asset's price will decline. The assets are sold at their current market value, and the proceeds from this sale are held by the investor.

4. Anticipating a Price Decline

The core belief in short-selling lies in the anticipation that the price of the sold assets will decrease. This anticipation is the driving force behind the entire short-selling strategy. Investors rely on their analysis of market trends, company performance, and other relevant factors to make informed predictions about the asset's future value.

5. Waiting for the Optimal Moment

Patience becomes a crucial virtue in short-selling. The investor monitors market conditions, economic indicators, and any factors influencing the asset's value. The goal is to identify the optimal moment to repurchase the borrowed assets at a lower price. Timing is paramount in maximizing potential profits.

6. Repurchasing at a Lower Price

When the anticipated decline in the asset's price occurs, the investor enters the market again, this time to repurchase the same quantity of assets that were initially borrowed and sold. The assets are repurchased at the current, lower market price.

7. Returning the Borrowed Asset

With the repurchased assets in hand, the investor returns them to the broker, completing the short-selling transaction. The return of the borrowed assets closes the short position. The profit or loss is calculated based on the difference between the selling price and the repurchase price, accounting for transaction costs and fees.

In essence, the mechanism of short-selling involves a strategic interplay of borrowing, selling, and repurchasing assets with the goal of profiting from a decline in their market value. This dynamic approach to the markets demands a sophisticated understanding of market trends, meticulous timing, and a disciplined strategy to navigate the complexities of short-selling successfully.

Parties Involved

Understanding the intricacies of short-selling requires a closer look at the key parties involved in this financial strategy. The short-selling process comprises the lender, borrower, and market participants, each playing a distinct role that contributes to the overall dynamics.

1. The Lender
The lender in a short-selling transaction is typically an entity that owns the assets being sold short. This could be an individual investor, institutional investor, or even a brokerage firm acting on behalf of its clients. The lender plays a crucial role by lending the securities to the borrower for a specified period. In return, the lender often receives a fee, enhancing the income generated from their investment portfolio.

2. The Borrower
The borrower, often an institutional investor or a hedge fund, is the party looking to profit from the anticipated decline in the value of the borrowed assets. To engage in short-selling, the borrower borrows the securities from the lender, with the obligation to return them at a later date. The borrower aims to sell these borrowed assets in the open market at the current market price, anticipating that their value will decrease. Once the price drops, the borrower buys back the assets at a lower cost, returning them to the lender and pocketing the difference as profit.

3. Market Participants
Apart from the lender and borrower, various market participants are involved in the short-selling process. These participants include other investors, traders, and market makers who engage in buying and selling the borrowed securities. Their actions influence the demand and supply dynamics in the market, contributing to the overall price movements of the short-sold asset.

4. Clearing Houses and Brokers

Clearing houses and brokers play a crucial role in facilitating and ensuring the smooth execution of short-selling transactions. They act as intermediaries, managing the exchange of securities between the lender and borrower, handling collateral, and ensuring that the transaction adheres to regulatory requirements. Brokers, on the other hand, assist borrowers in locating available securities to borrow and execute the necessary trades.

5. Regulatory Authorities

Regulatory authorities, such as the Securities and Exchange Commission (SEC) in the United States, oversee and regulate short-selling activities. They establish rules and guidelines to ensure fair and transparent markets, preventing practices like market manipulation or abuse of the short-selling strategy.

Understanding the roles of these key parties is crucial for investors and market participants seeking to navigate the complexities of short-selling. The collaboration and interactions among the lender, borrower, and other market participants create a dynamic environment that requires careful consideration and adherence to regulatory frameworks for the successful execution of short-selling strategies.

Key Components of Short-Selling

To grasp the operational dynamics of short-selling, it's crucial to delve into the key components that form the foundation of this intricate financial strategy. These components encompass various elements, including margin accounts and collateral, which play pivotal roles in facilitating and regulating short-selling transactions.

1. Margin Accounts

Margin accounts are fundamental to short-selling, allowing investors to borrow funds to finance their short positions. When an investor engages in short-selling, they typically open a margin account with their brokerage. This account enables them to borrow money against the value of their existing securities, providing the necessary capital to initiate the short sale. However, it's important to note that trading on margin involves additional risks, as losses can exceed the initial investment.

2. Collateral

Collateral serves as security for the lender in a short-selling transaction. When a borrower shorts a stock, they are essentially borrowing shares from the lender with the promise to return them at a later date. To secure this agreement, the borrower is often required to provide collateral, which can be in the form of cash, other securities, or even a portion of the proceeds generated from the short sale. Collateral acts as a safeguard for the lender, mitigating the risk associated with the borrower's obligation to return the borrowed securities.

3. Borrowing Costs

Borrowing costs are another key component of short-selling. Since the borrower is essentially renting the securities, they often incur fees for borrowing them from the lender. These fees, known as the "short interest rate" or "borrowing rate," are determined by market demand and supply for the specific securities being borrowed. High demand for a particular stock can result in higher borrowing costs.

4. Risk Management

Effective risk management is crucial in short-selling. Given that the potential losses in short-selling are theoretically unlimited (as the asset's price can rise indefinitely), investors must employ risk mitigation strategies. This can involve setting stop-loss orders to automatically close out the short position if the asset's price moves against them beyond a certain point, limiting potential losses.

5. Market Liquidity

Market liquidity is a significant consideration in short-selling. Highly liquid markets provide a smoother process for entering and exiting short positions, reducing the risk of price manipulation. Illiquid markets, on the other hand, can pose challenges, making it harder to execute trades at desired prices.

6. Regulatory Compliance

Adhering to regulatory requirements is a cornerstone of short-selling. Regulatory bodies, such as the SEC, have established rules to ensure fair and transparent markets. Investors engaging in short-selling must comply with these regulations to prevent market manipulation, maintain market integrity, and protect all stakeholders involved.

Exploring these key components provides valuable insights into the operational intricacies of short-selling. Margin accounts, collateral, borrowing costs, risk management, market liquidity, and regulatory compliance collectively shape the landscape within which short-selling transactions unfold. Investors navigating the world of short-selling must navigate these components judiciously to mitigate risks and optimize their investment strategies.

PART 3

RISKS ASSOCIATED WITH SHORT-SELLING

Engaging in short-selling introduces investors to a realm of challenges, and at the forefront of these challenges is the inherent market risk. Market dynamics play a pivotal role in determining the success or failure of short-selling strategies, making it imperative for investors to navigate these risks with caution and strategic acumen.

1. Volatility Impact
Markets are inherently volatile, and short-sellers are exposed to the unpredictable nature of price movements. Unlike traditional long positions where losses are capped at the initial investment, short-selling carries the potential for unlimited losses. Sudden and significant price fluctuations can lead to substantial losses for short-sellers, especially if the market moves against their anticipated direction.

2. Market Sentiment
Short-selling success is closely tied to market sentiment. If negative sentiment prevails, short-sellers may find favorable conditions for profiting from falling asset prices. However, shifts in sentiment, driven by unforeseen events or changing economic conditions, can swiftly turn the tide against short

positions. Recognizing and interpreting market sentiment is a continuous challenge for those engaged in short-selling.

3. Timing Challenges

The adage "timing is everything" holds particularly true for short-selling. Investors need to accurately predict when a particular asset's price will decline. Mistiming the market can result in significant losses, as short positions may be open for an extended period, accumulating losses until the anticipated price decrease occurs. This timing challenge adds complexity to short-selling strategies.

4. Liquidity Concerns

Liquidity, or the ease with which an asset can be bought or sold without affecting its price, is a critical factor in short-selling. Illiquid markets can amplify price movements and make it challenging for short-sellers to execute trades at desired prices. Moreover, low liquidity can lead to higher borrowing costs, impacting the overall feasibility of short-selling.

5. Unforeseen Events

Short-sellers are vulnerable to unexpected events that can swiftly alter market dynamics. Economic shocks, geopolitical events, or sudden changes in company fundamentals can trigger unforeseen price movements, catching short-sellers off guard. Adapting to and managing these unforeseen events requires a level of agility and resilience in short-selling strategies.

6. Regulatory Changes

Regulatory frameworks governing financial markets are subject to change. Alterations in rules related to short-selling can impact the feasibility and legality of established strategies. Short-sellers need to stay abreast of regulatory developments and adapt their approaches to comply with evolving market regulations.

7. Short Squeezes

Short squeezes occur when a heavily shorted stock experiences a rapid price increase, forcing short-sellers to cover their positions by buying back shares. This surge in buying activity can intensify price spikes, leading to substantial losses for short-sellers who are compelled to exit their positions at higher prices.

Navigating market risk in short-selling demands a comprehensive understanding of financial markets, a keen awareness of global economic factors, and the ability to adapt swiftly to changing conditions. While the potential rewards of successful short-selling can be significant, the associated market risks underscore the importance of a well-researched, strategic, and disciplined approach for investors venturing into this complex terrain.

Unlimited Losses

In the realm of short-selling, an inherent risk distinguishes itself starkly from traditional investing— the prospect of unlimited losses. Unlike the structured and capped risks associated with conventional investment strategies, short-selling introduces a unique challenge where losses can theoretically extend infinitely. Recognizing and mitigating this risk is paramount, requiring meticulous risk management practices for investors venturing into the world of short-selling.

1. The Nature of Unlimited Losses
Short-selling involves borrowing assets with the expectation that their value will decrease. However, if the market moves against the short-seller, the potential for losses is not capped. Unlike buying a stock where the maximum loss is the initial investment, short-selling exposes investors to a scenario where the asset's price can rise indefinitely, leading to escalating losses.

2. Risk Amplification
The nature of unlimited losses in short-selling is amplified by the concept of leverage. Investors often use borrowed funds (margin) to engage in short-selling, increasing the size of their position. While leverage can magnify profits, it also intensifies losses. If the market moves contrary to the short-seller's expectations, the borrowed funds contribute to the exponential growth of potential losses.

3. Market Reversals
Short-selling relies on accurate predictions of market movements. In the event of a sudden and unexpected market reversal, short-sellers can find

themselves in a precarious position. As prices surge upward, the losses for short-sellers accumulate, and the absence of an upper limit amplifies the financial impact.

4. Timing Risk

Timing is critical in short-selling, and mistiming the market can result in substantial losses. The longer a short position remains open, the greater the exposure to unlimited losses. Even a temporary surge in the asset's price can lead to significant financial setbacks for the short-seller.

5. Risk Management Imperative

Given the potential for unlimited losses, effective risk management becomes non-negotiable for those engaged in short-selling. Establishing clear stop-loss orders, which automatically trigger the closure of a short position if losses reach a predetermined threshold, is a fundamental risk mitigation strategy. These orders serve as protective mechanisms, limiting exposure to catastrophic financial consequences.

6. Constant Monitoring

Short-sellers must vigilantly monitor market conditions, company fundamentals, and broader economic trends. Continuous assessment helps identify potential risks and prompts timely adjustments to short positions. Remaining alert to changing market dynamics is instrumental in avoiding prolonged exposure to the risk of unlimited losses.

7. Diversification as a Safeguard

Diversification across different assets and markets can act as a safeguard against the risk of unlimited losses. Spreading short-selling activities across a well-diversified portfolio helps mitigate the impact of adverse price movements in a single asset.

The risk of unlimited losses in short-selling underscores the need for disciplined risk management practices. Investors must approach short-selling with a keen understanding of the associated risks, employ effective risk mitigation strategies, and remain adaptable in response to changing market conditions. While the potential rewards can be enticing, acknowledging and addressing the challenge of unlimited losses is essential for responsible and informed short-selling strategies.

Timing Risks

In the intricate dance of short-selling, the element of timing assumes paramount importance. Successfully navigating the waves of market movements demands an acute sense of timing. Misjudging these movements can swiftly translate into substantial financial setbacks for those engaged in short-selling, underscoring the critical nature of mastering the temporal nuances within this investment strategy.

1. Sensitivity to Market Trends
Short-selling is inherently sensitive to market trends, and timing is the linchpin that determines success or failure. The goal is to initiate short positions when a decline in asset prices is imminent. However, markets are dynamic, influenced by a myriad of factors, and predicting the precise moment when a price decline will occur is an intricate challenge.

2. Market Timing Complexity
The complexity of market timing is exacerbated by the unpredictable nature of financial markets. Economic indicators, geopolitical events, and unforeseen developments can swiftly alter market dynamics. Short-sellers must navigate these uncertainties, attempting to time their entries and exits with precision to maximize profits and minimize losses.

3. Long-Term vs. Short-Term Timing
Short-selling introduces the challenge of distinguishing between short-term and long-term market movements. Misjudging the duration of a downtrend can lead to premature exits or delayed entries, both of which can result in financial setbacks. The intricate balance between short-term fluctuations and overarching market trends requires a nuanced understanding of market behavior.

4. The Impact of Market Sentiment
Market sentiment plays a significant role in timing risks. Shifts in investor

sentiment can trigger abrupt changes in market directions. Short-sellers need to gauge and interpret sentiment accurately, anticipating potential shifts that may impact the timing of their short positions.

5. The Influence of External Factors

External factors, such as economic data releases, geopolitical events, or corporate developments, can exert sudden and profound effects on market dynamics. Short-sellers must be vigilant, considering these external factors in their timing strategies to avoid being caught off guard by unexpected events.

6. Risk Mitigation Through Research

Thorough research and analysis act as powerful tools for mitigating timing risks. Conducting comprehensive fundamental and technical analysis enables short-sellers to make informed predictions about market movements. The more informed the timing strategy, the better positioned the investor is to navigate the complexities of short-selling.

7. Continuous Monitoring

Given the fluid nature of financial markets, short-sellers must engage in continuous monitoring. Regularly reassessing market conditions and adjusting timing strategies in response to changing variables is integral to minimizing timing risks. This proactive approach allows for agile decision-making and reduces the likelihood of prolonged exposure to adverse market movements.

The challenge of timing in short-selling necessitates a combination of skill, research, and adaptability. Investors must recognize the intricacies of market behavior, stay attuned to evolving conditions, and continuously refine their timing strategies. While mastering timing in short-selling is undoubtedly a formidable task, the potential rewards for those who navigate these risks with finesse can be substantial.

Regulatory Risks

Amid the complexities of short-selling, investors face a distinct category of risks emanating from the regulatory landscape. Navigating the regulatory framework is not merely a compliance exercise; it is a critical aspect of managing the inherent risks associated with short-selling. Changes in rules and regulations can significantly impact the feasibility and legality of short-selling strategies, requiring investors to stay vigilant and adapt to evolving regulatory environments.

1. Dynamic Regulatory Environment

Regulatory frameworks governing financial markets are dynamic and subject to frequent revisions. Short-sellers must remain attentive to changes in rules and regulations imposed by regulatory bodies such as the Securities and Exchange Commission (SEC) in the United States or equivalent authorities in other jurisdictions. These changes can range from alterations in reporting requirements to more substantive shifts in the permissibility and restrictions on short-selling activities.

2. Impact on Feasibility

Regulatory changes have the potential to alter the feasibility of certain short-selling strategies. New restrictions or limitations imposed by regulators may constrain the ability of investors to engage in specific types of short-selling or introduce additional requirements, affecting the cost and operational aspects of implementing short positions.

3. Legal Compliance

Adherence to regulatory requirements is paramount for short-sellers. Failure to comply with established rules can result in legal consequences, including fines and penalties. Investors must stay informed about the legal framework within which they operate, ensuring that their short-selling activities align with current regulations to mitigate legal risks.

4. Reporting Obligations

Regulatory bodies often impose reporting obligations on short-sellers. This includes disclosing short positions and other relevant information to market authorities. Changes in reporting requirements can impact the transparency and disclosure practices of short-sellers, influencing market participants' perceptions and potentially affecting the success of short-selling strategies.

5. Global Regulatory Variances

Short-selling activities may extend across global markets, each governed by its regulatory framework. Investors engaged in cross-border short-selling must contend with regulatory variances, requiring a nuanced understanding of the diverse rules and compliance standards in each jurisdiction. Harmonizing short-selling strategies with global regulatory requirements becomes imperative in such scenarios.

6. Public Perception and Regulatory Scrutiny

Short-selling has, at times, faced scrutiny from regulatory bodies and public opinion. Regulatory changes influenced by public sentiment can impact the permissibility and conditions of short-selling. Investors need to navigate not only the letter of the law but also the broader sentiment and political climate surrounding short-selling activities.

7. Proactive Compliance Measures

Mitigating regulatory risks necessitates a proactive approach to compliance. Investors should implement robust internal controls and compliance measures, ensuring that their short-selling activities align with prevailing regulations. Regular reviews and updates to compliance protocols are crucial in a landscape where regulatory changes can occur with relative frequency.

Regulatory risks in short-selling underscore the importance of vigilance, adaptability, and a keen awareness of the legal landscape. Investors must proactively monitor and comply with regulatory changes, recognizing that effective risk management extends beyond market dynamics to include the evolving regulatory environment. By staying informed and responsive, investors can navigate the challenges posed by regulatory risks in the realm of short-selling.

PART 4

BENEFITS AND CONTROVERSIES

Hedge Against Market Downturns

In the dynamic landscape of financial markets, where uncertainties and downturns are inevitable, short-selling emerges as a strategic tool, offering a unique advantage as a hedge against market downturns. While traditional investments may falter during adverse market conditions, short-selling provides investors with a mechanism to potentially offset losses and even profit amid challenging economic climates.

1. Inverse Profit Potential
One of the primary benefits of short-selling as a hedge is its inverse profit potential. Traditional investments, such as long positions in stocks, may incur losses when market values decline. Short-selling allows investors to capitalize on falling asset prices, generating profits as the market experiences a downturn. This inverse relationship enhances the overall resilience of an investment portfolio.

2. Diversification Strategy
Short-selling contributes to portfolio diversification, a fundamental risk

management strategy. By incorporating short positions alongside traditional long positions, investors can create a more balanced portfolio. This diversification helps mitigate the impact of market downturns on the overall value of the portfolio, as gains from short positions can offset losses from traditional investments.

3. Risk Mitigation

During market downturns, many investors witness the erosion of value in their long positions. Short-selling offers a unique avenue for risk mitigation. By strategically selecting assets to short-sell, investors can create a counterbalance to their long positions. This hedging strategy acts as a safety net, limiting potential losses during turbulent market conditions.

4. Profiting from Bear Markets

Traditional investments often struggle in bear markets, where widespread pessimism prevails. Short-selling allows investors to not only protect their portfolio but also profit from the prevailing negative sentiment. Successfully shorting assets that experience significant declines can generate returns even when the broader market is on a downturn.

5. Strategic Asset Allocation

Short-selling facilitates strategic asset allocation based on market conditions. During periods of economic expansion and bullish trends, investors may focus on traditional long positions. In contrast, when signs of a market downturn emerge, strategically incorporating short positions can enhance the overall flexibility and adaptability of an investment strategy.

6. Adaptability to Changing Economic Conditions

The ability to short-sell provides investors with a tool to adapt to changing economic conditions. Economic cycles include both expansionary and contractionary phases. Short-selling empowers investors to navigate through these cycles actively, adjusting their portfolio to align with the prevailing market sentiment.

7. Risk Management in Uncertain Times

Uncertain economic times often accompany market downturns. Short-selling, as a hedge, becomes a valuable risk management tool in such periods.

It enables investors to take a proactive stance, identifying opportunities to profit from declining markets while safeguarding against potential losses in their long positions.

Short-selling's role as a hedge against market downturns highlights its strategic importance in risk management. By incorporating short positions, investors can diversify their portfolios, potentially profit from bear markets, and navigate the complexities of fluctuating economic conditions. This adaptability positions short-selling as a valuable tool for investors aiming to protect and optimize their portfolios in the face of market uncertainties.

Ethical Concerns

While short-selling provides investors with strategic tools to navigate financial markets, it is not without its ethical considerations. The practice often sparks debates about the morality of profiting from others' financial misfortune, raising important questions about the ethical implications embedded within short-selling strategies.

1. Profiting from Others' Losses
One of the primary ethical concerns associated with short-selling revolves around the notion of profiting from others' losses. In a short sale, gains for the short-seller typically translate to losses for the entity or individual holding the borrowed securities. Critics argue that this profit dynamic introduces a moral dilemma, as it seems to capitalize on the financial misfortune of others.

2. Market Manipulation Allegations
Short-selling has, at times, been accused of contributing to market manipulation. Critics argue that concerted short-selling activities can artificially drive down the price of a targeted asset, potentially leading to a self-fulfilling prophecy where the negative sentiment generates the very outcome short-sellers are betting on. Such perceived manipulation raises ethical concerns about fairness and market integrity.

3. Impact on Companies and Jobs
Short-selling can impact the companies whose stocks are targeted. A significant decline in stock prices may affect the financial health of these

companies, potentially leading to consequences such as layoffs or disruptions in operations. Ethical considerations come into play as short-sellers navigate the fine line between pursuing financial gains and potentially harming the real-world livelihoods of employees and stakeholders.

4. Information Asymmetry and Unfair Advantage

Ethical debates also center around information asymmetry. Short-sellers often conduct extensive research to identify overvalued assets. Critics argue that this information advantage may be unfair, as retail investors or those without access to such resources may be at a disadvantage. This ethical concern questions the fairness and inclusivity of market participation.

5. Fostering a Negative Market Sentiment

The act of short-selling inherently expresses a bearish view on specific assets. Critics contend that widespread short-selling can contribute to an overall negative market sentiment, potentially influencing other market participants and amplifying market downturns. This raises ethical questions about the responsibility of short-sellers in shaping market perceptions.

6. Regulatory Responses and Legal Boundaries

Regulatory responses to short-selling often involve a delicate balancing act. Regulators aim to address potential market abuses while preserving the integrity of markets. The ethical considerations arise in determining the appropriateness of regulatory measures and the establishment of legal boundaries that both support market efficiency and protect against unethical practices.

7. Transparency and Accountability

Ethical short-selling practices emphasize transparency and accountability. Investors engaged in short-selling should be transparent about their positions, adhere to regulatory reporting requirements, and act accountably to prevent potential abuses. Upholding these ethical principles contributes to maintaining market trust and integrity.

The ethical concerns surrounding short-selling underscore the need for a nuanced and principled approach to this investment strategy. Striking a balance between pursuing financial gains and maintaining ethical standards requires thoughtful consideration, transparency, and ongoing dialogue within the financial community and regulatory bodies. As the financial landscape evolves, addressing these ethical considerations becomes integral to ensuring the responsible and sustainable practice of short-selling in global markets.

PART 5

EXAMPLES OF SHORTING GONE WRONG

Famous Short-Selling Failures

Exploring historical instances of short-selling failures provides valuable insights into the consequences of overlooking associated risks. While short-selling can be a powerful strategy, history reveals instances where prominent investors and hedge funds faced significant setbacks due to miscalculations, market dynamics, or unexpected events.

1. The Volkswagen Short Squeeze (2008)
One of the most iconic short-selling failures occurred in 2008 when Porsche, in a surprising turn of events, disclosed that it held a significant stake in Volkswagen. This revelation triggered a massive short squeeze as short-sellers rushed to cover their positions. The sudden surge in demand for Volkswagen shares led to an unprecedented spike in their price, causing substantial losses for those who had bet against the automaker.

2. Tesla's Remarkable Ascent (2020)
Tesla, led by Elon Musk, experienced a remarkable ascent in 2020. Short-

sellers betting against the electric car company faced enormous losses as Tesla's stock price soared. Musk's influence, positive sentiment around electric vehicles, and strong financial performance defied expectations and left many short-sellers scrambling to cover their positions, underscoring the challenges of betting against high-profile companies.

3. The GameStop Saga (2021)
The GameStop saga of 2021 exemplifies the power of retail investors and the risks associated with heavily shorted stocks. An online community of individual investors, coordinated through platforms like Reddit's WallStreetBets, collectively drove up the stock price of GameStop, inflicting substantial losses on institutional short-sellers. The event highlighted the unpredictability of retail investor movements and the potential for short squeezes.

4. Herbalife Battle (2012-2018)
The Herbalife battle between activist investor Bill Ackman and investor Carl Icahn showcased the complexities of short-selling in the context of a high-profile corporate feud. Ackman publicly declared Herbalife a pyramid scheme and initiated a massive short position. However, Icahn took the opposite stance, leading to a public clash. Despite Ackman's persistence, Herbalife's stock did not collapse as he predicted, resulting in significant losses for his hedge fund.

5. Lehman Brothers (2008)
Short-selling played a role in the lead-up to the 2008 financial crisis, particularly with institutions like Lehman Brothers. While some investors successfully shorted Lehman's stock, the broader market turmoil and the subsequent bankruptcy of Lehman Brothers led to unprecedented challenges. Short-sellers faced both substantial gains and losses amid the tumultuous events of the financial crisis.

6. Overlooking Risks in Dot-Com Bust (2000)
During the dot-com era, many short-sellers targeted overvalued tech stocks. However, some failed to anticipate the speculative fervor that characterized the period. As the dot-com bubble burst, numerous short-sellers faced challenges as stock prices defied conventional valuations, leading to

unexpected losses.

Risk of Regulatory Actions

Short-sellers must also consider the risk of regulatory actions impacting their positions. Instances where regulatory scrutiny or interventions in response to short-selling activities have occurred highlight the need for thorough assessment and compliance with regulations.

Famous short-selling failures serve as cautionary tales for investors. These historical instances emphasize the importance of meticulous risk assessment, thorough research, and an awareness of broader market dynamics. Short-selling, while a potent strategy, requires a deep understanding of the risks involved, as overlooking these risks can lead to substantial financial setbacks. Learning from these failures is integral to cultivating a more nuanced and informed approach to short-selling in today's dynamic financial landscape.

Lessons Learned

Analyzing past failures in the realm of short-selling offers invaluable lessons for contemporary investors seeking to navigate the complexities of financial markets. These historical instances underscore the importance of strategic acumen, risk management, and adaptability in the pursuit of successful short-selling strategies.

1. Anticipate Unpredictability
One overarching lesson is the acknowledgment of market unpredictability. Historical short-selling failures often stem from unforeseen events, sudden shifts in sentiment, or unanticipated disclosures. Contemporary investors must recognize the inherent uncertainty in financial markets and factor unpredictability into their risk assessment models.

2. Diversify Short-Selling Strategies
The failures highlighted the risks associated with a one-size-fits-all approach to short-selling. Investors should diversify their short-selling strategies,

considering factors such as market conditions, asset classes, and risk tolerance. A well-diversified approach can help mitigate the impact of unexpected events on the overall short portfolio.

3. Adaptability in Dynamic Markets

Short-selling requires adaptability to evolving market dynamics. Lessons from failures emphasize the need to continuously reassess and adjust short positions in response to changing economic conditions, regulatory landscapes, and unexpected events. Investors who exhibit adaptability are better equipped to navigate the complexities of short-selling.

4. Thorough Due Diligence

Failures often result from inadequate research and due diligence. Contemporary investors must conduct thorough analyses of the assets they plan to short, considering both fundamental and technical factors. Understanding company fundamentals, market trends, and potential catalysts for price movements is crucial to making informed short-selling decisions.

5. Risk Management as a Priority

The importance of robust risk management practices cannot be overstated. Lessons from failures highlight the significance of setting clear stop-loss orders, diversifying portfolios, and incorporating risk mitigation strategies. Prioritizing risk management is key to protecting against the potential downside inherent in short-selling.

6. Consider Behavioral Factors

Behavioral factors, including market sentiment and the influence of retail investors, played pivotal roles in some short-selling failures. Contemporary investors should be attuned to the psychological aspects of market participants, recognizing that sentiment and collective behavior can impact short positions. Integrating behavioral analysis into decision-making processes enhances the effectiveness of short-selling strategies.

7. Continuous Monitoring and Oversight

The failures underscore the need for continuous monitoring and oversight of short positions. Markets evolve, and unexpected developments can unfold rapidly. Contemporary investors must remain vigilant, regularly reassessing their short portfolios, and staying informed about potential catalysts that could impact the success or failure of short-selling strategies.

8. Navigate Regulatory Landscape Prudently

Regulatory considerations played a role in several short-selling failures. Lessons learned highlight the importance of navigating the regulatory landscape prudently. Investors should stay informed about regulatory changes, comply with reporting requirements, and anticipate potential regulatory responses to short-selling activities.

The lessons learned from historical short-selling failures form a crucial guide for contemporary investors. By assimilating these lessons into their approach, investors can fortify their strategies, enhance risk management practices, and navigate the intricacies of short-selling with a more informed and resilient outlook. As financial markets continue to evolve, these lessons serve as beacons of wisdom for those aiming to master the art and science of short-selling.

PART 6

STRATEGIES FOR MITIGATING
SHORT-SELLING RISKS

Diversification

Diversifying one's portfolio stands as a proven and prudent strategy to effectively mitigate the inherent risks associated with short-selling. While short-selling can offer strategic advantages, it also exposes investors to unique challenges. Diversification serves as a powerful risk management tool, enabling investors to spread their exposure across various assets and market segments, reducing the impact of adverse movements in any single position.

1. Reducing Concentration Risk
Diversification in the context of short-selling helps alleviate concentration risk. By spreading short positions across different assets, industries, or sectors, investors avoid over-reliance on the performance of a single security. This strategic dispersion minimizes the impact of unfavorable developments in any specific market segment, safeguarding the overall portfolio.

2. Balancing Bullish and Bearish Views
Short-selling inherently reflects a bearish view on specific assets or markets.

Diversification allows investors to balance their overall portfolio by incorporating both long and short positions. This equilibrium enables them to navigate both bullish and bearish market scenarios, ensuring that the success of one aspect of the portfolio can offset potential losses in the other.

3. Sector and Industry Diversification

Beyond balancing long and short positions, diversification extends to sectors and industries. Focusing short positions on a variety of sectors reduces exposure to adverse developments specific to a particular industry. It acknowledges that economic conditions impact sectors differently, providing a hedge against sector-specific challenges.

4. Geographical Diversification

Geographical diversification is another facet of a well-rounded strategy. Short-selling across different geographic regions helps mitigate risks associated with regional economic downturns, political instability, or currency fluctuations. A globally diversified portfolio adds a layer of resilience, as economic conditions can vary significantly across borders.

5. Asset Class Diversification

Diversifying across asset classes broadens the scope of risk mitigation. Combining short positions in stocks with other asset classes, such as commodities or currencies, reduces vulnerability to market-specific events. Asset class diversification acknowledges that various financial instruments respond differently to economic conditions.

6. Factor-Based Diversification

Factor-based diversification involves considering various factors that influence asset prices. These factors can include market capitalization, valuation metrics, or momentum indicators. By diversifying short positions based on multiple factors, investors can enhance their ability to adapt to evolving market dynamics and reduce exposure to risks associated with a singular factor.

7. Dynamic Portfolio Adjustment

Diversification is not a static concept; it requires dynamic portfolio adjustment. Investors should regularly reassess their short positions, taking into account changes in market conditions, economic outlooks, and geopolitical factors. This proactive approach ensures that the portfolio remains aligned with the investor's risk tolerance and market expectations.

8. Risk-Return Optimization

Diversification is ultimately about optimizing the risk-return profile of a portfolio. While short-selling introduces specific risks, a diversified portfolio aims to strike a balance, allowing investors to capitalize on market opportunities while managing the potential downsides. The goal is to achieve a more stable and resilient investment strategy.

Diversification emerges as a cornerstone strategy for investors engaged in short-selling. By systematically spreading exposure across different assets, sectors, geographies, and factors, investors can navigate the challenges of short-selling while enhancing the overall robustness of their investment portfolios. This strategic approach not only mitigates risks but also positions investors to adapt to the dynamic and unpredictable nature of financial markets.

Stop-Loss Orders

Implementing stop-loss orders stands as a crucial risk management tool, particularly in the context of short-selling. This strategic approach enables investors to proactively limit potential losses, providing a mechanism to exit positions before significant damage occurs. Stop-loss orders are instrumental in mitigating the inherent uncertainties of short-selling, offering a predefined exit point that aligns with an investor's risk tolerance.

1. Defining Stop-Loss Orders

Stop-loss orders are predetermined instructions to sell an asset when its price reaches a specified level. In short-selling, this means automatically closing a short position if the asset's price rises to a predetermined threshold. By setting clear and enforceable stop-loss orders, investors establish a safety net that activates when the market moves against their short positions.

2. Limiting Downside Exposure

One of the primary advantages of stop-loss orders is their role in limiting downside exposure. Short-selling carries the risk of unlimited losses if the price of the borrowed asset rises indefinitely. Stop-loss orders act as a protective measure, automatically triggering the closure of the short position when losses reach a predefined level. This proactive approach helps investors contain potential financial setbacks.

3. Disciplined Risk Management

Stop-loss orders embody disciplined risk management. Investors set these orders based on a careful assessment of their risk tolerance and the specific dynamics of the short positions. This discipline ensures that emotions and market fluctuations do not drive impulsive decisions, fostering a structured and principled approach to managing short-selling risks.

4. Adaptability to Market Volatility

Markets can be volatile, and short-selling involves navigating price movements that may not always align with predictions. Stop-loss orders adapt to market volatility by adjusting to the prevailing conditions. Whether triggered by sudden market fluctuations or unexpected events, stop-loss orders provide a dynamic response to changing market dynamics.

5. Preventing Emotional Decision-Making

Emotional decision-making is a common pitfall in investing. Stop-loss orders act as a barrier against emotional reactions to market movements. Investors might be tempted to hold onto losing positions in the hope of a market reversal. Stop-loss orders, however, enforce a rational and predefined exit strategy, preventing impulsive decisions driven by fear or greed.

6. Facilitating Automated Execution

Stop-loss orders facilitate automated execution. Once the specified price level is reached, the order is automatically triggered, ensuring swift and seamless execution. This automation is particularly advantageous in fast-moving markets, where delays in execution could exacerbate losses.

7. Customization for Each Position

Investors can customize stop-loss orders for each short position, tailoring them to the unique characteristics of the asset and the investor's risk appetite. This granularity allows for a nuanced and strategic application of stop-loss orders across a diversified short portfolio.

8. Continuous Monitoring and Adjustment

The effectiveness of stop-loss orders relies on continuous monitoring and adjustment. Investors should regularly reassess market conditions and, if necessary, adjust the stop-loss levels based on new information or changing dynamics. This active management ensures that stop-loss orders remain aligned with the evolving market landscape.

Implementing stop-loss orders is a fundamental risk management practice for investors engaged in short-selling. By establishing clear exit points and embracing disciplined risk management, investors can navigate the challenges of short-selling with greater confidence and resilience. Stop-loss orders represent a proactive and strategic tool that not only limits potential losses but also contributes to a more systematic and informed approach to short-selling in dynamic financial markets.

Thorough Research

In-depth research stands as a paramount practice for investors engaged in short-selling. The success of short-selling strategies hinges on a comprehensive understanding of the financial health of a company and the broader market trends. Thorough research not only informs the decision to initiate a short position but also positions investors to navigate the complexities of short-selling with heightened awareness and strategic acumen.

1. Analyzing Financial Health

Thorough research begins with a meticulous analysis of the financial health of the company targeted for short-selling. Investors delve into financial statements, cash flow reports, and balance sheets to assess the company's solvency, profitability, and overall financial stability. This deep dive provides insights into potential vulnerabilities that may make the company a suitable candidate for short-selling.

2. Evaluating Profitability Metrics

Profitability metrics are integral components of research. Short-sellers scrutinize metrics such as profit margins, return on equity (ROE), and earnings per share (EPS). These metrics offer a nuanced perspective on the company's ability to generate profits and its overall financial performance. Deviations from industry standards or historical averages can signal potential weaknesses.

3. Understanding Debt Levels

A critical aspect of research involves understanding the debt levels of the targeted company. Investors assess the company's debt-to-equity ratio and debt servicing capabilities. Elevated levels of debt, especially when coupled with challenging market conditions, can expose a company to financial stress, making it a plausible candidate for short-selling.

4. Market Trends and Industry Analysis

Successful short-selling requires a holistic view of market trends and industry dynamics. Thorough research extends to analyzing broader economic trends and the specific conditions within the industry in which the targeted company operates. A deteriorating industry outlook or systemic challenges can further support the rationale for initiating short positions.

5. Monitoring Management Practices

Research encompasses an evaluation of management practices and corporate governance. Investors scrutinize the decisions and strategies implemented by the company's leadership. Instances of questionable governance or decisions that may compromise long-term sustainability can influence the decision to pursue short-selling opportunities.

6. Utilizing Technical Analysis

Technical analysis complements fundamental research by examining historical price movements and market trends. Short-sellers employ tools such as charts, trend lines, and technical indicators to identify potential entry and exit points for short positions. Technical analysis adds a quantitative dimension to research, enhancing decision-making precision.

7. Assessing Short Interest and Sentiment

Research extends to assessing short interest and overall market sentiment regarding the targeted company. High short interest may indicate a consensus among investors about potential weaknesses. However, investors must also be aware of the contrarian nature of markets, where excessively negative sentiment could lead to short squeezes.

8. Scenario Analysis and Contingency Planning

Thorough research involves scenario analysis and contingency planning. Short-sellers anticipate various scenarios, considering both favorable and unfavorable outcomes. This proactive approach enables investors to adapt their strategies based on evolving market conditions, minimizing the impact of unforeseen events.

9. Continuous Information Flow

Research is not a one-time effort but a continuous process. Short-sellers stay attuned to news, market updates, and corporate developments that may impact their positions. Continuous information flow ensures that short positions remain aligned with the latest market intelligence and evolving circumstances.

Thorough research is the bedrock of successful short-selling. Investors who commit to a comprehensive understanding of the financial landscape, market trends, and industry dynamics position themselves to make informed decisions. Beyond initiating short positions, ongoing research enables investors to adapt to changing conditions, navigate uncertainties, and optimize their short-selling strategies for sustained success in the dynamic realm of financial markets.

PART 7

SHORT-SELLING IN DIFFERENT MARKETS

Short-Selling in Stock Markets

Understanding how short-selling operates in stock markets is essential for equity investors seeking a comprehensive grasp of market dynamics. Short-selling, a nuanced and strategic practice, involves selling borrowed securities with the anticipation that their prices will decline, allowing the investor to repurchase them at a lower cost. This process provides unique insights into market behavior and offers both risks and opportunities for investors navigating the world of equities.

1. Initiating a Short Position
Short-selling in stock markets begins with the initiation of a short position. An investor borrows shares from a broker and sells them in the open market. The goal is to repurchase the same shares at a later date, ideally at a lower price, and return them to the lender, profiting from the price difference.

2. Market Dynamics and Price Decline Anticipation
Short-sellers actively analyze market dynamics and assess factors that may contribute to a decline in a stock's price. This analysis can involve

fundamental research, technical analysis, and an understanding of broader economic trends. Short-sellers anticipate price declines and strategically time their short positions to capitalize on market movements.

3. Risk and Reward Scenario

Short-selling introduces a distinct risk and reward scenario for investors. While the potential for profit exists if the stock's price decreases, the risk is unlimited if the price rises. Investors must carefully manage their positions, utilizing risk mitigation strategies such as stop-loss orders to limit potential losses.

4. Bearing the Cost of Borrowing

Short-selling involves borrowing shares, and this borrowing comes at a cost. Investors engaging in short-selling typically pay fees for borrowing shares, contributing to the overall cost of the short position. The cost of borrowing is an additional factor that investors must consider when evaluating the feasibility of short-selling strategies.

5. Short Squeezes and Market Volatility

Short-selling activities can contribute to market volatility and, at times, lead to short squeezes. A short squeeze occurs when the price of a heavily shorted stock rises sharply, prompting short-sellers to cover their positions by buying back shares. This rush to cover positions can further drive up the stock's price, creating a volatile cycle.

6. Regulatory Framework

Short-selling is subject to regulatory frameworks designed to maintain market integrity. Regulations may include disclosure requirements, restrictions on "naked" short-selling (selling shares without actually borrowing them), and measures to address potential market abuses. Investors engaging in short-selling must adhere to these regulations.

7. Impact on Market Efficiency

Short-selling plays a role in market efficiency by contributing to price discovery. Short-sellers, through their analysis and actions, provide a counterbalance to optimistic market sentiments. This dynamic interaction between long and short positions contributes to a more nuanced and reflective pricing mechanism in stock markets.

8. Role in Active Portfolio Management

Short-selling serves as a tool for active portfolio management. Investors use short positions to hedge against market downturns, generate returns in bearish conditions, and diversify their portfolios. This strategic application of short-selling aligns with broader portfolio management objectives.

9. Educational Value for Investors

Understanding how short-selling operates in stock markets offers educational value for investors. It provides insights into market psychology, risk management strategies, and the interplay between different market participants. This knowledge enhances an investor's ability to make informed decisions and navigate the complexities of equity markets.

10. Contributing to Market Liquidity

Short-selling contributes to market liquidity by increasing the number of available shares for trading. This liquidity is essential for the smooth functioning of stock markets, allowing investors to buy and sell shares more efficiently.

Comprehending the intricacies of short-selling in stock markets is crucial for equity investors. It goes beyond a mere trading strategy, offering a deeper understanding of market dynamics, risk management practices, and the role of different market participants. Armed with this knowledge, investors can approach the world of equities with a more informed and strategic perspective, positioning themselves to make well-calculated decisions in both bullish and bearish market conditions.

Shorting in Cryptocurrency Markets

The burgeoning cryptocurrency market introduces unique challenges and opportunities for short-sellers, offering a distinctive landscape compared to traditional equity markets. Shorting in cryptocurrency markets involves betting against the value of digital assets, and understanding the intricacies of this practice is essential for investors seeking to navigate the evolving world of cryptocurrencies.

1. Digital Asset Dynamics

Shorting in cryptocurrency markets revolves around digital assets, such as Bitcoin, Ethereum, and a myriad of altcoins. Unlike traditional stocks, these digital assets are decentralized, borderless, and often driven by technological advancements, regulatory shifts, and community sentiment. Short-sellers must grasp the unique dynamics that influence cryptocurrency prices.

2. Leveraging Crypto Exchanges

Cryptocurrency short-selling is facilitated through specialized crypto exchanges. Short-sellers borrow digital assets from these platforms, sell them in the market, and aim to repurchase them at a lower price. The availability of leverage on certain exchanges enhances the potential returns but also amplifies risks, requiring cautious risk management.

3. Volatility as a Constant

Cryptocurrency markets are renowned for their volatility. Prices can experience significant fluctuations within short timeframes, creating both opportunities and risks for short-sellers. Understanding and embracing the inherent volatility is crucial for devising effective short-selling strategies in the cryptocurrency space.

4. Short Squeezes and Liquidity Challenges

Short squeezes, a phenomenon familiar in traditional markets, also occur in cryptocurrency markets. Rapid price increases can force short-sellers to cover their positions quickly, exacerbating upward price movements. Liquidity challenges may arise, especially in less liquid altcoins, impacting the ability to execute trades efficiently.

5. Regulatory Dynamics

Cryptocurrency markets operate in a dynamic regulatory environment. Regulatory changes, announcements, or developments can significantly impact prices. Short-sellers must stay abreast of regulatory dynamics globally, considering the potential influence on market sentiment and the feasibility of short-selling strategies.

6. Technological Factors

Technological advancements play a pivotal role in cryptocurrency markets. Changes or upgrades to blockchain technology, security concerns, or innovations in decentralized finance (DeFi) can influence the value of digital assets. Short-sellers need to consider the technological landscape when assessing potential short positions.

7. Community Sentiment

Cryptocurrency prices are often influenced by community sentiment. Social media platforms, forums, and online communities play a crucial role in shaping perceptions and driving price movements. Short-sellers should monitor and analyze community sentiment to gauge potential shifts in market dynamics.

8. Diversification in Crypto Shorts

Diversification remains a key strategy for short-sellers in cryptocurrency markets. Given the variety of digital assets available, shorting a diversified portfolio can help spread risk. However, careful consideration of each asset's unique characteristics is essential to effectively manage exposures.

9. Risk Management in Crypto Shorts

Robust risk management practices are paramount in cryptocurrency short-selling. Volatility, leverage, and the 24/7 nature of crypto markets demand disciplined risk mitigation. Stop-loss orders, position sizing, and continuous monitoring are critical components of effective risk management in the crypto space.

10. Evolution of Cryptocurrency Derivatives

The evolution of cryptocurrency derivatives, including futures and options, has expanded the toolkit for short-sellers. These instruments offer additional avenues for expressing short positions, allowing investors to tailor their strategies based on market expectations and risk preferences.

Shorting in cryptocurrency markets is a dynamic and evolving practice that requires a nuanced understanding of digital assets, technological shifts, and market sentiment. While presenting unique challenges, the cryptocurrency space also offers opportunities for investors to capitalize on price movements and diversify their portfolios. Armed with a deep understanding of the cryptocurrency landscape, short-sellers can navigate this complex market with agility and strategic acumen.

Short-Selling in Real Estate

Real estate markets, typically associated with property ownership and long-term investments, are not exempt from the realm of short-selling strategies. Exploring this niche provides investors with a holistic view of investment possibilities, showcasing a distinctive approach to navigating the complexities of the real estate landscape.

1. The Essence of Real Estate Short-Selling
Short-selling in real estate involves speculating on the decline in the value of a property. Unlike traditional real estate investments where investors aim for property appreciation, short-sellers anticipate a decrease in property values, enabling them to profit from the price differential.

2. Shorting Real Estate Investment Trusts (REITs)
Real Estate Investment Trusts (REITs) are commonly targeted by short-sellers. REITs are publicly traded companies that own, operate, or finance income-producing real estate. Short-sellers may engage in bearish bets on REITs, anticipating adverse market conditions that could impact the underlying real estate assets.

3. Utilizing Real Estate Derivatives
Short-selling in real estate is facilitated through derivatives, including real estate options and futures. These financial instruments allow investors to express bearish views on real estate markets without directly owning the physical property. Real estate derivatives provide flexibility and leverage for short-selling strategies.

4. Economic and Market Indicators
Short-sellers in real estate closely monitor economic and market indicators. Factors such as interest rates, employment levels, and housing market trends

influence property values. Thorough analysis of these indicators guides short-sellers in identifying potential opportunities and risks within the real estate sector.

5. Identifying Overvalued Markets

Short-selling in real estate often involves identifying overvalued markets. Short-sellers scrutinize property markets where prices may be inflated relative to economic fundamentals. This analysis can include factors such as excessive speculation, high levels of debt, or unsustainable price appreciation.

6. Evaluating Macro and Microeconomic Trends

Successful real estate short-selling requires a comprehensive evaluation of both macro and microeconomic trends. Macro trends, such as national economic indicators, interest rate policies, and demographic shifts, interact with micro trends like local employment rates and housing supply, influencing property values.

7. Market Timing and Cyclical Trends

Timing is critical in real estate short-selling. Investors aim to capitalize on cyclical trends within real estate markets. Identifying inflection points in the market cycle, such as the peak of a housing bubble, allows short-sellers to strategically enter positions before potential downturns.

8. Risks and Considerations

Short-selling in real estate comes with inherent risks. Unlike stocks or cryptocurrencies, physical properties involve tangible assets, making the short-selling process more complex. Investors must consider factors like property maintenance, regulatory changes, and the potential for unforeseen events impacting property values.

9. Impact of External Factors

Real estate short-sellers are attuned to the impact of external factors on property values. These factors may include changes in zoning laws, environmental regulations, or shifts in local economies. External influences can alter the dynamics of real estate markets, creating opportunities for short-selling strategies.

10. Diversification in Real Estate Shorts

Diversification remains a fundamental strategy for short-sellers in real estate. By shorting across different property types, regions, or real estate sectors, investors can spread risk and optimize their short positions based on a nuanced understanding of diverse market dynamics.

Short-selling in real estate introduces a nuanced dimension to traditional property investment strategies. While less common than in financial markets, the practice allows investors to capitalize on bearish views and navigate the cyclical nature of real estate markets. By leveraging derivatives, monitoring economic indicators, and identifying overvalued markets, short-sellers in real estate contribute to the diversified landscape of investment possibilities.

PART 8

REAL-LIFE STORIES

Investor Experiences with Short-Selling

Embarking on the journey of short-selling is akin to navigating uncharted waters, and the tales of investors who have successfully traversed this challenging terrain serve as beacons of inspiration and guidance for those venturing into the world of bearish bets. These firsthand accounts offer a glimpse into the mindset, strategies, and hard-earned wisdom that define the experiences of successful short-sellers.

1. Risk Perception and Gut Instinct
Seasoned short-sellers often emphasize the role of intuitive risk perception. Hearing how successful investors developed a keen sense for identifying overvalued assets, understanding market dynamics, and gauging potential downturns provides aspiring short-sellers with valuable insights into the intuitive aspects of risk management.

2. In-Depth Research as a Cornerstone
Across these narratives, a common thread is the unwavering commitment to in-depth research. Successful short-sellers stress the importance of thorough analysis, scrutinizing financial reports, assessing industry trends, and staying

abreast of macroeconomic factors. The experiences highlight that research is not just a step but a cornerstone for effective short-selling strategies.

3. Discipline in Execution
Short-selling demands discipline in execution, and hearing how investors adhered to predefined strategies, set stop-loss orders, and resisted emotional impulses adds a layer of practical wisdom. These experiences underscore the significance of maintaining a structured approach even in the face of market fluctuations.

4. Patience Amidst Market Volatility
The narratives delve into the virtue of patience when engaged in short-selling. Investors recount instances where they weathered market volatility, allowing their bearish bets to unfold over time. Patience emerges as a vital ingredient for success, counteracting the urge to succumb to short-term market noise.

5. Adaptability to Changing Conditions
Short-selling success stories often revolve around adaptability. Investors share how they adjusted their strategies as market conditions evolved, demonstrating the need for flexibility. These experiences highlight that rigid adherence to a single approach may not suffice in the dynamic landscape of short-selling.

6. Risk Management and Contingency Planning
Risk management is a recurring theme in these narratives. Successful short-sellers stress the importance of setting clear risk thresholds, utilizing stop-loss orders, and incorporating contingency plans. Learning from their experiences, investors emphasize the need for a robust risk management framework to navigate the uncertainties inherent in short-selling.

7. Balancing Conviction and Humility
The experiences of short-sellers showcase a delicate balance between conviction and humility. Investors share instances where unwavering conviction in their analysis led to profitable outcomes, but they also acknowledge the humility required to reassess positions when faced with unexpected market movements or new information.

8. Continuous Learning and Adaptation

The journey of short-selling is marked by a commitment to continuous learning. Investors recount how each trade, whether successful or challenging, contributed to their growth. These experiences underscore that the ability to adapt, learn from mistakes, and refine strategies is essential for longevity and success in the field.

9. Mental Resilience and Emotional Control

Short-selling is a mentally demanding endeavor, and the narratives delve into the importance of emotional control. Investors share how they developed resilience in the face of market uncertainties, setbacks, and the psychological challenges associated with betting against conventional market optimism.

10. Sharing the Human Side of Investing

Beyond strategies and market dynamics, the experiences shared by investors provide a human perspective on the world of short-selling. These narratives humanize the often complex and technical aspects of investing, making the journey relatable for those considering or actively engaged in short-selling.

The narratives of investors who have successfully navigated short-selling offer more than just financial insights. They provide a glimpse into the human elements of investing—courage, resilience, adaptability, and a perpetual thirst for knowledge. Aspiring short-sellers can draw inspiration and practical wisdom from these experiences, fostering a deeper understanding of the challenges and rewards that characterize the world of bearish bets.

PART 9

REGULATORY MEASURES AND OVERSIGHT

SEC Regulations

In the complex landscape of financial markets, understanding the regulatory framework is crucial, especially when it comes to engaging in short-selling. The Securities and Exchange Commission (SEC) plays a pivotal role in overseeing and regulating securities activities in the United States. Navigating the regulatory waters, particularly the guidelines set by the SEC, is essential for compliance, ethical conduct, and effective risk mitigation in the realm of short-selling.

1. Overview of the SEC
The Securities and Exchange Commission, established in 1934, is a key regulatory body tasked with maintaining fair and efficient markets. The SEC's mission is to protect investors, facilitate capital formation, and ensure the integrity of the securities markets through effective regulation and enforcement.

2. Disclosure Requirements
The SEC imposes stringent disclosure requirements to ensure transparency

in financial markets. Companies engaging in short-selling activities or providing related services are obligated to disclose pertinent information to the public. Investors and market participants rely on these disclosures to make informed decisions.

3. Short Sale Reporting

SEC regulations mandate the reporting of short sale transactions. Broker-dealers are required to submit regular reports detailing short sale activities, contributing to the SEC's oversight of market dynamics. This reporting requirement aids in monitoring potential market abuses and maintaining market integrity.

4. Rule 201 (Alternative Uptick Rule)

The SEC has implemented Rule 201, also known as the Alternative Uptick Rule, to address concerns related to short-selling during periods of market stress. This rule aims to curb excessive volatility by imposing restrictions on short selling when a stock experiences a significant price decline.

5. Regulation SHO

Regulation SHO is a set of SEC rules governing short sales and stock borrowing. It includes provisions to address concerns like naked short selling—selling shares without actually borrowing them. The regulation establishes procedures for marking sales as "short," ensuring compliance with borrowing and delivery requirements.

6. Anti-Fraud and Market Manipulation Enforcement

The SEC actively enforces regulations against fraud and market manipulation. Short-sellers must adhere to ethical practices, avoiding false or misleading statements that could manipulate market perceptions. Enforcement actions are taken against those engaging in fraudulent activities to maintain market integrity.

7. Proxy Rules

SEC proxy rules govern the disclosure of information by companies and individuals seeking to acquire more than 5% of a company's securities. Short-sellers involved in activities that could influence corporate control must comply with these rules, contributing to transparency and informed decision-making.

8. Insider Trading Prohibitions

Short-sellers must adhere to SEC prohibitions on insider trading. Information obtained through illegal means or deemed non-public is not to be used for trading purposes. The SEC actively investigates and takes legal action against individuals or entities engaging in insider trading practices.

9. Global Reach of SEC Regulations

While the SEC primarily oversees U.S. securities markets, its regulations can have extraterritorial effects. Foreign entities engaging in activities that impact U.S. markets or American investors may be subject to SEC regulations. This global reach reinforces the SEC's commitment to maintaining the integrity of U.S. financial markets.

10. Educational Initiatives

The SEC undertakes educational initiatives to inform investors about the risks and benefits of short-selling. Educational materials and resources are provided to help market participants understand the intricacies of short-selling, fostering a more informed and resilient investor community.

Understanding SEC regulations is fundamental for anyone involved in short-selling activities. The SEC's regulatory framework aims to protect investors, ensure fair markets, and prevent fraudulent activities. Compliance with these regulations not only mitigates risks for market participants but also contributes to the overall stability and trustworthiness of the financial markets. As the SEC continues to adapt to evolving market dynamics, market participants must stay abreast of regulatory changes to navigate the complex terrain of short-selling responsibly and ethically.

Global Regulatory Framework

Engaging in short-selling on a global scale demands a keen awareness of the diverse regulatory environments that govern financial markets. Each country or region has its own set of rules and regulations, creating a complex mosaic of compliance requirements. Navigating this intricate web of global regulatory frameworks is essential for market participants involved in short-selling practices, ensuring adherence to legal standards and ethical conduct.

1. Regional Disparities in Regulations
The global regulatory landscape is characterized by regional disparities in regulations governing short-selling. Different countries may have distinct rules regarding disclosure requirements, permissible short-selling practices, and enforcement mechanisms. Market participants must be cognizant of these disparities to operate within legal boundaries.

2. EU Short-Selling Regulation
In the European Union (EU), short-selling activities are subject to specific regulations outlined in the EU Short-Selling Regulation. This framework aims to enhance transparency by requiring the disclosure of significant short positions and facilitating coordination among EU member states to address risks associated with short-selling.

3. Asian Markets Regulatory Variances
Asian markets, including those in China, Japan, and South Korea, each have their own regulatory variances concerning short-selling. These regulations may include restrictions on naked short-selling, disclosure requirements, and specific rules to address market manipulation. Understanding these nuances is vital for market participants operating in Asian markets.

4. UK Financial Conduct Authority (FCA) Rules
The UK, a prominent financial hub, follows the regulatory guidelines set by the Financial Conduct Authority (FCA). These rules encompass various aspects of short-selling, emphasizing transparency and ensuring that market participants adhere to ethical practices. Any changes in FCA rules can significantly impact short-selling strategies in the UK.

5. Canadian Securities Administrators (CSA) Guidelines
Canada, like many other countries, has its own regulatory body overseeing securities activities. The Canadian Securities Administrators (CSA) provides guidelines and regulations related to short-selling practices. Market participants operating in Canada must comply with these regulations to maintain market integrity.

6. Australian Securities and Investments Commission (ASIC) Oversight

In Australia, short-selling activities fall under the oversight of the Australian Securities and Investments Commission (ASIC). ASIC regulates and enforces rules related to short-selling, aiming to foster fair and transparent markets. Understanding ASIC guidelines is crucial for those involved in short-selling in the Australian market.

7. Emerging Market Regulatory Challenges

Emerging markets often present unique regulatory challenges. Regulatory frameworks may be less established or subject to rapid changes. Market participants engaging in short-selling in emerging markets must stay vigilant, adapting to evolving regulatory landscapes and potential uncertainties.

8. Collaborative Regulatory Initiatives

Recognizing the interconnected nature of global financial markets, regulatory bodies engage in collaborative initiatives. Organizations such as the International Organization of Securities Commissions (IOSCO) work to establish common principles and standards, fostering a more harmonized global regulatory framework for short-selling activities.

9. Impact of Cross-Border Trading

Cross-border trading, a common practice in global markets, adds complexity to short-selling regulations. Market participants need to navigate the implications of trading securities across different jurisdictions, considering the regulatory requirements of both the origin and destination markets.

10. Compliance Technology and Reporting Systems

To navigate the global regulatory framework efficiently, market participants often leverage compliance technology and reporting systems. These tools help ensure adherence to diverse regulatory requirements, streamline reporting processes, and enhance transparency in cross-border short-selling activities.

Understanding the global regulatory framework is imperative for market participants engaged in short-selling on an international scale. Navigating the diverse regulations demands vigilance, adaptability, and a commitment to ethical conduct. By staying informed about regional disparities, collaborating with regulatory bodies, and leveraging technology for compliance, market participants can navigate the complex terrain of global short-selling with diligence and integrity.

PART 10

HOW SHORT-SELLING AFFECTS THE ECONOMY

Impact on Market Stability

Understanding the impact of short-selling on market stability is essential for gaining insights into its broader economic implications. While critics argue that short-selling can introduce volatility and destabilize markets, a closer examination reveals a more nuanced relationship.

Introduction to Market Dynamic

Short-selling is an integral part of market dynamics, providing a counterbalance to traditional buying strategies. It allows investors to express bearish views on assets, fostering a market environment where both bullish and bearish sentiments coexist.

Volatility vs. Stability

Contrary to common belief, short-selling can contribute to market stability by preventing the formation of speculative bubbles. When overvalued assets face short-selling pressure, it acts as a corrective force, aligning asset prices more closely with their intrinsic values. This, in turn, reduces the likelihood of abrupt, unsustainable market fluctuations.

Efficient Price Discovery

Short-selling enhances price discovery mechanisms in financial markets. By allowing investors to bet against overpriced assets, it helps reveal more accurate valuations. This process of efficient price discovery contributes to a healthier and more stable market environment over the long term.

Risk Mitigation and Hedging

Short-selling also serves as a risk mitigation tool. Investors engage in short-selling to hedge their portfolios against potential losses during market downturns. This strategic use of short-selling can contribute to overall market stability by providing a means for investors to protect themselves from adverse market conditions.

Regulatory Safeguards

Regulatory frameworks play a crucial role in ensuring that short-selling activities do not compromise market stability. Stringent regulations and monitoring mechanisms are in place to prevent market manipulation and excessive speculation. These safeguards aim to maintain a fair and orderly market while allowing the beneficial aspects of short-selling to thrive.

Educating Market Participants

Enhancing awareness and understanding among market participants about the role of short-selling can contribute to a more stable financial landscape. Education empowers investors to make informed decisions, reducing the potential for panic-driven market reactions.

Exploring how short-selling influences market stability reveals a multifaceted relationship. While it can introduce short-term volatility, its role in preventing market bubbles, facilitating efficient price discovery, and providing risk mitigation tools contributes to a more stable and resilient financial ecosystem. Acknowledging these dynamics is crucial for policymakers, investors, and the public to form a comprehensive view of short-selling's impact on market stability.

Role in Efficient Market Functioning

Short-selling, often viewed through a critical lens, plays a pivotal and constructive role in maintaining market efficiency. It serves as a mechanism that allows investors to express bearish views on assets, contributing to the overall equilibrium of financial markets. Understanding the multifaceted role of short-selling is essential for appreciating its impact on market dynamics and efficiency.

1. Price Discovery Mechanism
Short-selling acts as a vital component in the price discovery mechanism. By allowing investors to bet against the market, short-selling provides a counterbalance to optimistic sentiment. The resulting price movements reflect a more nuanced and balanced view of the actual value of assets, contributing to efficient market pricing.

2. Efficient Allocation of Capital
Short-selling facilitates the efficient allocation of capital by allowing investors to redirect resources away from overvalued assets. This process ensures that capital flows towards opportunities with stronger fundamentals, aligning with market realities. In essence, short-selling helps prevent asset bubbles and promotes a more rational allocation of resources.

3. Risk Mitigation and Portfolio Diversification
Investors engaging in short-selling effectively mitigate risk and diversify their portfolios. Short positions act as a hedge against market downturns, offering protection when traditional long investments may face challenges. This risk-mitigating aspect contributes to a healthier and more resilient financial ecosystem.

4. Enhanced Liquidity
Short-selling enhances market liquidity by introducing more trading activity. The ability to both buy and sell securities, whether through traditional long positions or short positions, fosters a more dynamic marketplace. Increased liquidity provides investors with improved execution of trades and contributes to the overall smooth functioning of financial markets.

5. Discourages Market Manipulation

Short-selling acts as a deterrent to market manipulation. The ability to bet against an asset's performance introduces a counterforce to speculative activities that may artificially inflate prices. This discouragement of manipulation promotes fair play and integrity within financial markets.

6. Correction of Overvaluation

In instances where assets are overvalued, short-selling serves as a corrective force. By betting against overvalued stocks or other securities, short-sellers can contribute to a correction, bringing prices more in line with underlying fundamentals. This correction is instrumental in preventing market bubbles and subsequent crashes.

7. Market Efficiency Through Informational Content

Short-selling adds informational content to markets. Investors who take short positions often conduct extensive research and analysis to identify weaknesses in companies or markets. The insights gained from this due diligence contribute valuable information to the broader market, enhancing overall efficiency.

8. Encourages Corporate Governance

The presence of short-selling can incentivize companies to uphold strong corporate governance practices. Knowing that their performance is subject to scrutiny from both long and short investors, companies are encouraged to maintain transparency, accountability, and effective management practices.

9. Adaptive Market Responses

Short-selling allows markets to adapt quickly to changing economic conditions or unforeseen events. If negative information emerges, short-sellers can respond by taking positions that reflect a pessimistic outlook, influencing prices to align with the new information. This adaptability contributes to the resilience of financial markets.

10. Facilitates Dynamic Investment Strategies

Investors employing short-selling strategies can engage in dynamic and proactive investment approaches. The ability to profit from falling asset prices enables a more versatile toolkit for investors, fostering innovation in investment strategies and contributing to the evolution of financial markets.

Short-selling, when conducted responsibly within the bounds of regulatory frameworks, plays an integral role in the efficient functioning of financial markets. Its contributions to price discovery, risk management, liquidity, and market integrity collectively shape a more resilient and adaptive marketplace. Recognizing the constructive aspects of short-selling provides a more nuanced perspective on its role in maintaining a healthy and efficient financial ecosystem.

PART 11

COMMON MISCONCEPTIONS

Short-Selling vs. Market Manipulation

One common misconception surrounding short-selling is the confusion between legitimate short-selling and market manipulation. Short-selling is a well-established financial strategy where investors capitalize on anticipated price decreases. However, some critics argue that short-selling can contribute to market manipulation, fostering a negative perception of this practice.

To address this misconception, it's essential to distinguish between the two. Market manipulation involves intentionally inflating or deflating the price of a security, creating a false appearance of market activity. Legitimate short-selling, on the other hand, is grounded in research and analysis, driven by the investor's belief in an asset's overvaluation.

Short-Selling and Economic Health

Another prevalent misconception revolves around the belief that short-selling negatively impacts economic health. Critics argue that by betting against companies, short-sellers undermine confidence and potentially contribute to economic downturns. However, a more nuanced perspective reveals that short-selling plays a vital role in market efficiency.

Short-selling provides a mechanism for investors to express bearish views on assets. This process, when conducted responsibly, can contribute to the correction of overvalued stocks, promoting a healthier and more accurate reflection of market conditions. Rather than being detrimental, short-selling can enhance market transparency and prevent the formation of asset bubbles.

By dispelling these misconceptions, investors and the general public can gain a more balanced understanding of short-selling's role in the financial ecosystem. It is crucial to acknowledge that, like any investment strategy, short-selling requires responsible and informed execution to mitigate potential risks and contribute positively to market dynamics.

PART 12

CURRENT TRENDS AND FUTURE OUTLOOK

Short-selling in modern financial markets

The landscape of short-selling has undergone significant transformations in tandem with the evolution of modern financial markets. Examining contemporary trends not only sheds light on the intricacies of this age-old practice but also reveals the profound impact of technology and changing market dynamics on short-selling strategies.

1. Electronic trading platforms

The advent of electronic trading platforms has revolutionized short-selling. Traders can now execute short orders swiftly and efficiently, leveraging advanced algorithms for precise timing. This shift from traditional manual processes to electronic platforms has enhanced the speed and accessibility of short-selling activities.

2. Algorithmic and high-frequency trading

Algorithmic and high-frequency trading have become integral to modern short-selling strategies. Complex algorithms analyze vast datasets, identifying potential shorting opportunities in real-time. High-frequency traders execute numerous short trades within fractions of a second, capitalizing on market inefficiencies and fleeting opportunities.

3. Big data analytics

Big data analytics play a crucial role in contemporary short-selling practices. Traders harness the power of vast datasets to uncover patterns, correlations, and signals that may indicate potential market movements. This data-driven approach enhances the precision of short-selling strategies, enabling more informed decision-making.

4. Machine learning and artificial intelligence

Machine learning and artificial intelligence (ai) have become indispensable tools for short-sellers. These technologies can analyze vast amounts of historical data, learn from patterns, and adapt strategies based on evolving market conditions. Machine learning algorithms enhance the predictive capabilities of short-selling models.

5. Real-time market information

The availability of real-time market information has transformed the way short-sellers operate. Traders can access up-to-the-minute data on asset prices, market trends, and news, allowing for timely adjustments to short positions. Real-time information contributes to agility and responsiveness in executing short-selling strategies.

6. Social media and sentiment analysis

Short-sellers now incorporate social media and sentiment analysis into their strategies. Monitoring online conversations and sentiment surrounding a particular asset provides additional insights. Traders can gauge public perception and factor sentiment analysis into their decision-making process, adding a qualitative dimension to short-selling.

7. Regulatory changes and reporting
Modern short-selling is subject to evolving regulatory frameworks. Changes in regulations, such as enhanced reporting requirements, aim to promote transparency and mitigate potential risks associated with short-selling. Traders must navigate these regulatory landscapes to ensure compliance and ethical conduct.

8. Cryptocurrency short-selling
The rise of cryptocurrencies has introduced a new dimension to short-selling. Traders can now engage in short-selling activities within cryptocurrency markets, betting on the price decline of digital assets. Cryptocurrency exchanges facilitate these transactions, creating unique opportunities and challenges for short-sellers.

9. Global interconnectedness
Modern financial markets exhibit a higher degree of global interconnectedness. Short-sellers must consider the impact of international events, economic indicators, and geopolitical developments on their positions. The interconnected nature of markets requires a more holistic approach to short-selling strategies.

10. Environmental, social, and governance (esg) factors
contemporary short-selling strategies increasingly incorporate environmental, social, and governance (esg) factors. Investors assess the sustainability and ethical practices of companies before engaging in short-selling activities. Esg considerations have become integral to evaluating the long-term viability of short positions.

Short-selling in modern financial markets is a dynamic and technologically influenced practice. The integration of electronic platforms, algorithmic trading, big data analytics, and emerging technologies has reshaped the landscape. Traders navigating this evolving terrain must adeptly leverage technological advancements while also considering the ethical implications and regulatory nuances that govern contemporary short-selling strategies.

Evolving strategies and technologies

The ever-changing landscape of financial markets is undergoing a transformative shift driven by the advent of new technologies. As we stand at the intersection of innovation and finance, the evolution of short-selling strategies is being profoundly shaped by cutting-edge technologies, offering a glimpse into the future of financial markets.

1. Quantitative trading models

The rise of quantitative trading models is at the forefront of evolving short-selling strategies. These models utilize mathematical and statistical techniques to identify patterns and execute trades with precision. As computing power continues to advance, quantitative strategies in short-selling gain sophistication and accuracy.

2. Blockchain and smart contracts

Blockchain technology, synonymous with cryptocurrencies, is making inroads into short-selling. The transparency and immutability inherent in blockchain offer new possibilities for creating smart contracts related to short positions. This technology can streamline processes, reduce counterparty risk, and enhance the efficiency of short-selling transactions.

3. Decentralized finance (FeFi)

The emergence of decentralized finance (DeFi) platforms introduces alternative avenues for short-selling. DeFi protocols leverage blockchain and smart contract technologies to create decentralized lending and borrowing platforms. Short-selling activities can occur in a decentralized, permissionless environment, challenging traditional financial intermediaries.

4. Predictive analytics and forecasting tools

Predictive analytics and advanced forecasting tools are becoming integral to short-selling strategies. Traders leverage machine learning algorithms to analyze vast datasets, identify trends, and make predictions about future market movements. This data-driven approach enhances decision-making in short-selling activities.

5. Robotic process automation (rpa)

Robotic process automation (rpa) is streamlining operational processes in short-selling. Repetitive tasks, such as data entry and trade execution, can be automated through rpa, freeing up human resources for more strategic decision-making. This technology contributes to operational efficiency and reduces the margin for human error.

6. Regtech solutions

Regulatory technology (regtech) solutions are aiding short-sellers in navigating the evolving regulatory landscape. Automated compliance checks, real-time monitoring, and enhanced reporting capabilities are facilitated by regtech tools. These solutions ensure that short-selling activities align with the ever-changing regulatory requirements.

7. Augmented reality (ar) in research

Augmented reality (ar) is influencing the research phase of short-selling. Analysts can use ar to visualize complex financial data, market trends, and macroeconomic indicators. This immersive technology enhances the depth of analysis, providing a more comprehensive understanding of the factors influencing short-selling decisions.

8. Crowdsourced intelligence platforms

Crowdsourced intelligence platforms are gaining prominence in short-selling research. Traders can tap into the collective insights of a diverse group of contributors to inform their short-selling strategies. These platforms leverage the wisdom of the crowd, potentially uncovering unconventional perspectives and market insights.

9. Cybersecurity measures
The increasing reliance on technology necessitates robust cybersecurity measures in short-selling activities. Traders and platforms need to safeguard sensitive data, prevent unauthorized access, and ensure the integrity of transactions. Cybersecurity becomes a critical component in maintaining trust and security within the short-selling ecosystem.

10. Environmental and social impact assessment tools
Short-sellers are incorporating tools that assess the environmental and social impact of targeted companies. As environmental, social, and governance (esg) considerations become more prominent, these tools aid in evaluating the sustainability and ethical practices of potential short positions, aligning with evolving market expectations.

The convergence of evolving strategies and technologies is reshaping the landscape of short-selling. From advanced quantitative models to blockchain innovations and decentralized finance, these developments signify a future where technology plays a central role in shaping short-selling strategies. As we embrace this era of transformation, adaptability and a forward-looking mindset become paramount for those navigating the ever-evolving intersection of finance and technology.

PART 13

IN CONCLUSION

Recap of Short-Selling and Its Risks

In wrapping up our exploration of short-selling, it is crucial to recognize this investment strategy as a nuanced and sophisticated approach to financial markets. Short-selling, the practice of betting against the upward trajectory of an asset, offers unique opportunities but is not without its challenges. As we recap, it becomes evident that a comprehensive understanding of the associated risks is paramount for anyone considering or engaged in short-selling activities.

Short-selling introduces a counterbalance to the traditional "long" investment strategy, allowing investors to profit from falling prices. However, the risks are inherent and multifaceted. From market dynamics and unlimited loss potential to regulatory uncertainties and timing risks, short-sellers operate in a landscape where challenges and complexities demand a meticulous approach.

Importance of Informed Investment Decisions

The journey into short-selling is a journey into the unknown, and it is the responsibility of investors to navigate this terrain with utmost care. Informed decision-making emerges as the guiding principle, emphasizing the need to balance potential rewards with the intricacies of associated risks. This balance requires a commitment to thorough research, market awareness, and adaptability in the face of evolving conditions.

As investors delve into short-selling, the importance of staying abreast of regulatory changes cannot be overstated. Compliance with regulatory frameworks, whether set by the Securities and Exchange Commission (SEC) or other global regulatory bodies, is not only a legal obligation but a safeguard against potential pitfalls.

In conclusion, short-selling, when approached with diligence and a well-informed perspective, can be a valuable tool in an investor's toolkit. However, the path is fraught with challenges that demand respect and strategic acumen. The risks associated with short-selling are not deterrents but rather navigational markers guiding investors towards a more nuanced understanding of the financial markets.

As we embrace the complexities and opportunities of short-selling, the call to action is clear: prioritize informed decision-making, cultivate resilience in the face of setbacks, and remain adaptable to the ever-evolving landscape of financial markets. Through these principles, investors can embark on the journey of short-selling with a measured confidence, ready to navigate the complexities and contribute to the vibrant and dynamic tapestry of the financial world.

ABOUT THE AUTHOR

Damien Soitout is a French businessman, investor and philanthropist.

He is the owner of the CPF Group based in the US, France and Mexico, with experience, expertise and success in 9 industries.

He has worked with some of the largest groups in the world, and has supported thousands of entrepreneurs and dreamers achieve their professional and personal goals through personalized programs, consulting, and free online content.

One of his missions is to open the minds of people with ambitious goals to organize their projects in such a way that they do not risk paying the Dumb Tax.

www.ingramcontent.com/pod-product-compliance
Lightning Source LLC
Chambersburg PA
CBHW071213290526
45796CB00008B/225